# All About

# PATTERN

# All About
# PATTERN

by Irene Yates
Illustrated by Jill Newton

 Belitha Press

First published in Great Britain in 1997 by
Belitha Press Limited,
London House, Great Eastern Wharf
Parkgate Road, London SW11 4NQ

Reprinted 1998

Series designer: Hayley Cove
Series editor: Maria O'Neill
Editor: Mary-Jane Wilkins

ISBN 1 85561 568 1 (hardback)
ISBN 1 85561 774 9 (paperback)

Printed in Hong Kong

British Library Cataloguing
in Publication Data
for this book is available
from the British Library.

# Contents

# What is pattern?

Patterns are all around us. Once you start to look for them you see them everywhere.

This is a pattern wheel. It has a stripy pattern, a herringbone pattern, checks, spots, a wavy pattern and a pattern of curves.

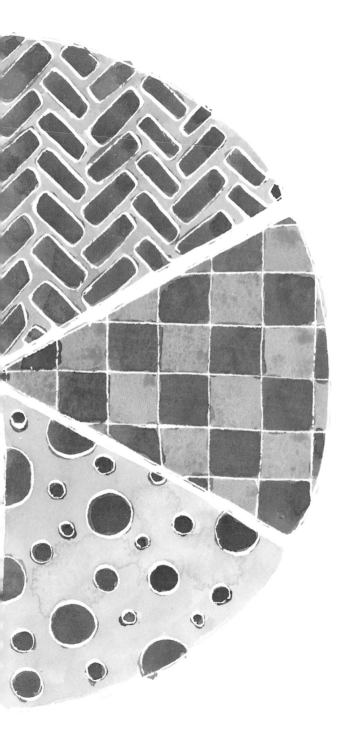

You will find patterns
on your clothes and
in your home.

This is a plain sock.

This is a patterned sock.
Which do you like best?

# Making patterns

Patterns are ways of arranging shapes or colours. When a shape or colour is repeated it becomes a pattern.

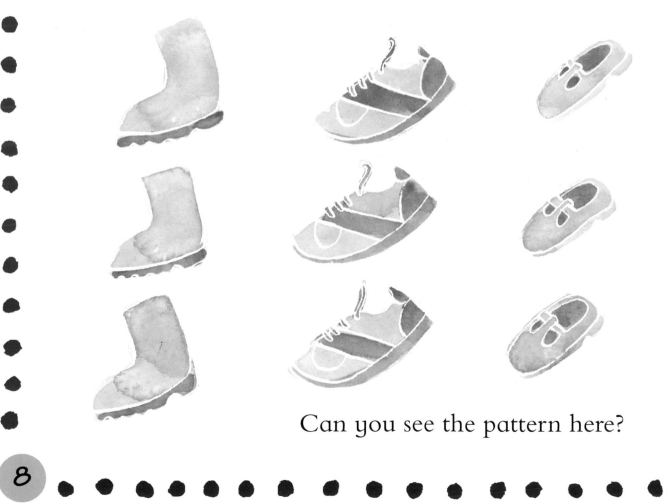

Can you see the pattern here?

There are two
patterns here.
Can you see
what they are?

What is the
pattern here?

# Lines

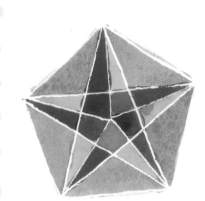

Straight lines can be arranged into patterns of stripes, checks and squares.

Can you see the stripes of the zebra? Are they straight or curved? Can you see other patterns of lines?

Small pieces of tile fit together to make a pattern called a mosaic.

A pagoda has a pattern of lines.

## Cut a pattern

Fold some paper in half, then in half again. Fold it again to make a triangle. Cut shapes from the folds and the open top. Open out the paper.

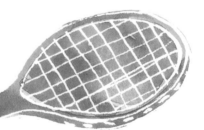

A racket has a pattern of straight lines inside a curved shape.

# Curves

Curved lines and circles make many different patterns. They can fit together to form new shapes.

How many different circle patterns can you see? Can you see something with curved and straight lines?

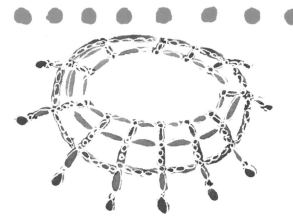

Beads are threaded into patterns to make jewellery.

**Fingerprint patterns**
Make fingerprints by pressing your thumb into some poster paint and pressing it on paper. Ask your friends to do the same.

A cobweb is a spiral. The spider builds straight lines, then goes round from the centre.

These fossils are ammonites. They were creatures with spiral shells which lived in the sea millions of years ago.

# Animal patterns

The patterns on animals help them to hide from enemies or to find a mate.

How many stripy patterns can you see? How many spotty patterns? Can you name all the creatures?

When a tiger hides
in the long grass, its
pattern looks the same
as the grass. The tiger
is camouflaged.

**Paint an animal**
Choose one of the animals
on this page and paint a
picture of it. Try to hide
it in its background.

The pattern on
a butterfly's wings
is very beautiful.

Angelfish know each
other by their stripes.

# Plant patterns

Have you seen any of the plants or flowers on these pages? Do you know their names?

Can you see an umbrella plant? Are there the same number of leaves on each branch?

**Grow a pattern.**
Draw a wiggly line across one corner of a sheet of paper. Draw another line following the same shape. Fill the whole sheet. Colour your pattern.

The spots on lily petals attract insects. The insects go into the flowers to gather nectar.

Mazes are puzzle patterns made with plants. The puzzle is to find your way out once you are inside.

Dandelion petals form a pattern. The seedheads also make a pattern.

# At home

People decorate
their clothes
and homes with
colourful patterns.

Look at the patterns on
these pages. Which do
you like best? Which do
you like least? Are there
patterns on your clothes?

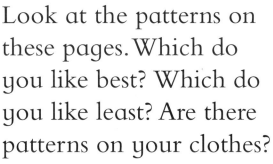

Rugs and carpets often have colourful patterns.

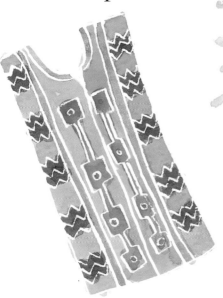

This cool, patterned tunic is worn in hot countries. It is called a jellabah.

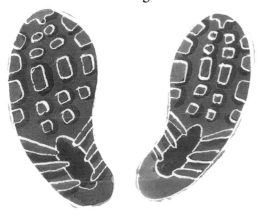

**Collect patterns**
Collect different fabric and paper patterns. Keep scraps of them in a photo album.

The patterns on cups and saucers often match to show that they belong together.

# Buildings

There are patterns in buildings. Some are for decoration, but others are useful.

Can you see an overlapping pattern? Can you see some patterns of curves?

**Go on a pattern walk.**
Take a pencil and paper
with you on a walk.
Draw the patterns you like.
Find at least ten patterns.

Overlapping patterns
are useful. Roof tiles
overlap to keep the
house dry.

Bridges are a way
of crossing from
one place to another.

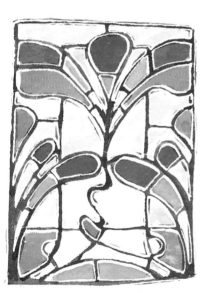

Pieces of coloured glass are
joined with lead to make
stained-glass windows.

# In the street

There are lots of patterns in the street, though you may not have noticed them.

Can you see patterns with curved and straight lines? Can you see a pattern with more than one shape?

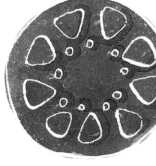

If you look at
a row of houses
you can see
many patterns.

## Draw a street pattern

Draw your pattern as
if you are looking down
on the street from above.
Put in roads, roundabouts,
buildings and trees.

Car wheels
have patterns
on them. When
the car moves the
patterns disappear.

The thick ridges on
tyres leave strong patterns
in mud or soft ground.

# At the shops

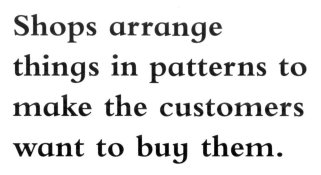

Shops arrange things in patterns to make the customers want to buy them.

Can you see an overlapping pattern on the fruit stall? How many different fruits can you name?

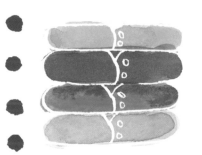

## Stacking patterns

When you go shopping look for eight new patterns in the colours, shapes and the ways things are stacked. Draw them.

When you look at all these rolls of fabric together you can see they make a pattern.

Crusty French loaves make a pattern of upright lines.

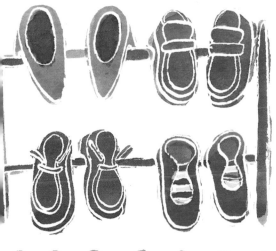

These beach balls make a pattern of curves piled inside a wire basket.

# Letter patterns

Capitals and small letters can be fitted together in different ways to make patterns.

How many different letters can you find here? Can you see letters that are upside down or back to front?

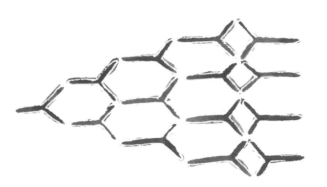

## Lines of letters

Fill a line with a letter, then turn the page round and write another line. Turn and write letters until the page is filled.

Letters that are all the same size and thickness make good patterns.

Look for the shapes that appear between the letters.

Find shapes that stay the same when you turn them round or flip them over.

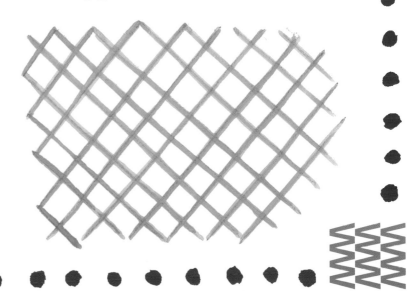

# Explore pattern

## Make a spiral

1 Cut out a small circle of paper.
2 Start from the centre and draw a line round and round until you reach the edge.
3 Colour the spaces.
4 Cut along the line.
5 Thread some cotton through the centre and hang up your spiral.

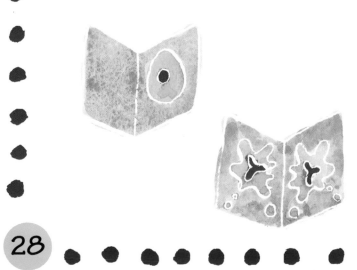

## Reflections

Fold a sheet of paper. Open it up. Put a blob of paint on one side of the fold. Fold and press the paper. Open it to see the pattern you have made.

## Printing patterns

You can print patterns
with these things and thick
poster paint. Dip your
object into the paint and
then press it on a piece
of paper. What happens
if you turn your object
round? What happens
if you turn it over?

# Picture list

**Here is a list of the pictures in this book.**

**Lines**  Star shape, triangle pattern, check pattern, starfish, zebra, railings, fan, mosaic, pagoda, Afro comb, tennis racket.

**Curves**  Curved patterns, fingerprint, scaly fish, tree trunk, wagon wheel, bead necklace, feather, cobweb, fossils.

**Animal patterns**  Tabby cat, lizard, caterpillar, peacock, leopard, giraffe, tiger, butterfly, angelfish, dalmatian.

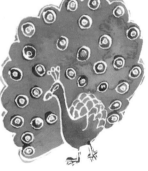

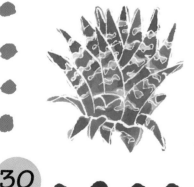

**Plant patterns**  Pine cone, tulips, umbrella plant, ivy leaves, partridge-breasted aloe plant, fern, cow parsley, lilies, hedge maze, dandelion flower, dandelion seedhead.

**At home** Basket, checked shorts, bobble hat, stripy trousers, saucepans, spotted T-shirt, lamp, rug, jellabah, trainer soles, cups and saucers.

**Buildings** Iron gate, herringbone brick pattern, log cabin, skyscraper, picket fence, steps, roof tiles, bridge, stained-glass window, castle.

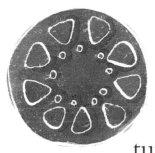

**In the street** Rainbow, row of trees, train carriages, telegraph poles, road markings, manhole cover, row of houses, car wheels, tyre tracks, car transporter.

**At the shops** Tins, bottles, pencils, cardigans, flowers, fruit, fabric rolls, French loaves, shoes, beach balls.

**Letter patterns** Letter Y, letter A, letter X, letter Z, letter V.

# Words to remember

**ammonite**  a creature with a spiral shell which lived millions of years ago.
**attract**  to make an animal come to a plant or another animal.
**camouflage**  colours and patterns on an animal that help it to hide in its surroundings.
**decorate**  to make something look special by adding colours and patterns.
**mate**  an animal of the same breed. Two animals mate to have young.
**mosaic**  a pattern made of small pieces of coloured glass, tile or stone.
**pagoda**  a tall temple.
**spiral**  a curved line that starts from a point and winds round and round.